MW00932101

Colloquial
ELEMENTS

Other Titles by J Christian Connett

Principles of Digital Marketing

6 Days in The City

I AM: inspired, aware, motivated

Coming soon: **Butterfly Sunset**

Colloquial ELEMENTS

*A Collection of Words, Prose,
Thoughts, & Quotes*

J Christian Connett

forvera
media

ISBN-13: 978-1-5423-6612-0
ISBN-10: 1542366127

Layout, Copy Editing & Design by Christian Connett
Published by Forvera Media

This book can be made available at special discounts when purchased in bulk for fund-raising or other approved use. Special editions can also be created by request. Other titles are available by the author.
Contact Forvera Media – info@christianconnett.com

FOR VERA

This work is dedicated to Vera A. Connett for believing in me when I was young, and encouraging me to live to the fullest, to watch the Sparrows and Swallows fly. She told me to make something of myself, and I have lived a lifetime of making something.

This work is also dedicated to someone that inspired me to write and live, more than ever, and encouraged me to be the best that I can despite all odds. She stood beside me and pushed me, loved me, and shared my dream. To Taylor Steffens for putting up with me and loving me without question or conjecture.

All my works, writing, and books are dedicated to my
three beautiful, intelligent, and magnificent daughters:
Kaitlynn, Madison, and Savanah.
I love you more than words can express.

ACKNOWLEDGMENTS

This book came about because of sharing many quotes, thoughts and random prose with friends, family, and acquaintances over the last year. I have received heartfelt gratitude, appreciation and thank you notes from many readers and follower. I am eternally grateful to those that continue to read my madness and motivation. To those that gave me the early vision to see the potential of this book.

Taylor Steffens, for her gracious and selfless love and adoration for my passion and our life together.

Che Connett, my Brother and his loving family, for never letting me quit, for keeping me focused on the good, and for introducing me to Taylor.

Connie Luffy for her undying love, adoration and support of my writing, my music, and my life.

Andrew Schwarz for always pushing me, editing, assisting, motivating, and leading me to greater aspirations.

Shannon Giles for being my confidante, friend, and honesty when I needed it.

Damon Moreno for the relentless pushing and encouraging attitude and helping to drive me to success.

James-Simon Schmidt who always had faith and shares my affinity for motivation, inspiration, and self-awareness.

Kate Davis for having such an amazing high spirit and deep understanding of life and unyielding friendship.

Connie Senn for holding me to faith and friendship and us each pushing one another beyond the past.

Tammy Simpson for the spiritual enlightenment, faith, and encouragement to stay happy and positive.

Tammi Gonzalez for the friendship and motivating conversations. Your faith and hope are contagious.

Additional thanks to Kris Alvarez, Mariah Andreasen, Donnie & Suzy Bensley, Ameela Ever Bless, Janel Burke, Vanessa Burnett, Suezet Cain, Angela Casey, Kristal Ann Churchill, Rhonda Glaspie, Jaque Harmon, Angel Hartman, Jolena Irving, Jenny St John, Shelly Pence, Amy Reidel, Lucas Sampson, Amber Showers, Christine Steeples, Debbie & Junior Steffens, Jenn Thompson, Greg & Susan Wright

INTRODUCTION

I share these with you, in hopes of sharing my inner workings and what motivates me. There is a great deal of emotion and passion put into these words. The excerpts from my books, social posts, and personal thoughts reveal some of the introspection, as well the depth of feeling the respective books convey.

I hope to inspire, motivate, and encourage you as you read these words, to know that you are not alone in your own thinking and feeling. We are all emotional and thought-filled creatures of humanity.

Please enjoy reading these, as I have enjoyed writing them and sharing them with you here within these pages. My heart, passion, tears, joy, and experiences unfold before you now.

The first two pages are some of my favorite quotes that I have enjoyed the last 12 months, in one way or another. They are property and copyright of their respective owners. I do not claim them as my own, I am simply sharing them with you here.

There are many quotes and passages from my two books – **6 Days in The City**, and **I AM: inspired, aware, motivated**. There are also random passages from my social media posts, memes, and other random thoughts.

"Life is 10% what happens to you,
and 90% how you react to it"
– Charles Swindoll.

"The only thing you ever have is now."
- Eckhart Tolle

"Life's tragedy is we get old too soon and wise too late."
- Benjamin Franklin

"Some of the most beautiful things worth having in your
life come wrapped in a crown of thorns."
- Shannon L. Alder

"We can complain because rose bushes have thorns, or
rejoice because thorn bushes have roses."
- Abraham Lincoln

"Those who do not move, do not notice their chains." -
Rosa Luxemburg

"There isn't any questioning the fact that some people enter your life, at the exact point of need, want or desire - it's sometimes a coincidence and most times fate, but whatever it is, I am certain it came to make me smile."
- Nikki Rowe

"I wasn't looking for anything when I found you
& it somehow made me question what I wanted,
was i ready for love? I don't think anyone is ever ready,
but when someone makes you feel alive again
it's kind of worth the risk..."
- Nikki Rowe

"For last year's words belong to last year's language,
and next year's words await another voice.
And to make an end is to make a beginning."
- T.S. Eliot

"Without music, life would be a mistake."
- Friedrich Nietzsche

Life happens no matter what, and we must embrace it as it comes. Always remember that life is perception and that every day is a new day.

It is never too late to start over,
which is precisely what I want you to do.
Right now.

Make today the memory
that you smile about in the future.

Inosculation will reveal beauty intertwined with adoration.

Please remember,
you are as beautiful as the stars in the night sky.

The relationships we develop define who we are.

Transformation is a process, not a destination.

Balance makes us one with ourselves.

Make the most out of each breath you take.

I am not living my life for you.
I am living my life for me.

Sometimes we have to brave the storm to see the rainbow on the other side.

To know where you are,
you must know WHO you are.
To know where you've been,
you must know WHO you are.

My heart is in my family.
They are my reasons to breathe.

Sometimes there is no glass to fill.
You must rebuild, reshape, rediscover.

Leave the past behind you, it is time to move forward. You cannot move forward by ruminating and thinking backward. The past will always be a part of you, but it will never define who you are.
Take that next step.

If you continue to bleed for everyone else, you will bleed yourself dry. Remember to love and cherish others, but don't forget about yourself.

You are not the mistakes you have made.

Most days I challenge myself;
Some days I'm just challenged.

Often life is not as we expected.
Embrace the changes and roll with the waves.

Beauty is where you find it.

Life is perception.

Be who you are.
Be the best you that you can be.

Great success is borne of great failure.

We have to get through the things that we don't like, to get to the things that we do like.

Stand up and dream for yourself.

Be the foundation of your success. Build your life from your own foundation, don't wait for anyone else to do it for you. Don't wait until the "time is right", because the right time is right now... You are responsible for your own success, and it begins each day with you.

The following are passages from my book **6 Days in The City – One Man's Journey of Self-Discovery**. They are pulled directly from the book. Many of these deal with low self-esteem and depression.

6 Days in The City tells the story of a man dealing with a failing marriage, and suffering from a sense of low self-worth and low self-esteem, while discovering himself through introspection and temptations while on a business trip to San Francisco.

J CHRISTIAN CONNETT

So here I was, on the edge of a fantasy; bordering
divorce, sanity and the uncanny feeling
of being lost in another world.

I never enjoyed being away from home, or my girls. But
when I was gone, it was as if they were all somehow
better off without me.

It was never really about me, or her. It was about being
alone, even when we were together.

Perhaps God was, for some unknown reason, looking at me, smiling and thinking, 'how can I challenge him?'. All the while knowing that I could handle it; unbeknownst to me.

Normal is something that some asshole made up
because he or she couldn't explain something
that they didn't understand. It's easier to
claim that it's normal or not normal.

What else was there?
I had looked into myself many times,
not that it showed or told me any damned thing
that I needed to know at that point.

I felt alone, utterly and sickly alone.
I don't think anyone else knows what I feel.
Men aren't supposed to feel like little
bitchy boys with self-esteem issues.
But, that is exactly how I felt sometimes.

My one true passion is my music.

Life has mysterious oddities that transcend in and out of my mind that drive me nuts sometimes. We are all crazy; we just choose to show it off in different ways.

I enjoyed the fact that as I walked around,
I could see and feel eyes staring at me.

Sometimes I would just enjoy having a companion
to share some thoughts with,
and hold conversation without judgment.

Again, I questioned, who am I?

Every day that I woke,
I would look straight out the window,
from my bed, and view the beautiful mountains
that were seemingly right outside the window. It would
bring me some sort of peace and solace in that moment.

Somehow, the perfect opportunity seems to just come out of nowhere.

I am truly lost within myself, and beside myself.
No wonder I question my motives in life.

It's almost easy to discuss other people's problems
and issues, but when it comes to intervening
with your own story, things get reactive.

You will have to make decisions that change you, and they are not the easy ones, no matter what you decide.

This was it, and I had to make the right decision,
either way, it was not going to be easy,
but it was going to be the best,
because I had to make the decision
that was truly in my heart...

The following passages are from my book **I AM: inspired, aware, motivated** – True stories of overcoming abuse, heartache, & self-indulgence.

Writing this book brought out some of the most raw and unedited writing that I have ever committed to paper.

I had a lot of emotions and thoughts racing while I continued the evolution of this book. I am proud of the outcome, it shows how much time and effort that I put forth, not only in my personal education, but as a person overall.

I culminated some of my most memorable pieces from the book and I am sharing them with you.

In survival mode, I need to push myself harder
than ever because, in the end, this will be
a story I tell - not the way I live.

I walked away from it all. I had to. I had to discover who I was inside of me, from the bottom to the top, inside and out. I needed to essentially pull down all the walls and learn how to rebuild them again.

I had to reevaluate my entire life, my complete being,
to fully understand what pieces needed improving,
and what pieces could remain.

It has been very difficult, some days more than others. But now I am standing, breathing, and taking life day by day and embracing it for what it is.

The storms we weather make us stronger,
and we are never the same person
when we come out the other side…

My words and thoughts are brought to life by many experiences and the knowledge that I have learned.

Too many people spend too much time trying to impress everyone in the room, they forget to impress themselves.

Demeanor defines a person's character instantly.

It was a defining moment in some aspects because I discovered that I had an ability to drive myself to the edge of my mind and sanity.

The key to it all, was the breathing.
In through the nose, our through the mouth.
Eventually I learned to count the seconds.
3 and 7 seem to be my favorable numbers,
so I would draw a breath in and slowly count to 3…
As I would exhale and slowly count to 7.
This has helped many times bring my heart rate
back to normal, and calm my body and mind.

I loved the sound of the needle touching down
on the record, excitedly anticipating the aural energy
that would emerge from the turntable.

It was divinity and levity that nothing else could replace.
I would turn to music over and over again in my life.
It was my saving grace.

Once we gain enough knowledge to make
the best choices for ourselves, we are held
responsible for what we do and what we feel.

Things happen, words, situations,
and happy or sad –
they are going to continue to happen to us.
It is purely how we ourselves react to those
situations that create the best result of our lives.

I am not perfect, none of us on this earth are perfect.
We are constantly learning.
I am still learning and practicing how to be better
than I was the day before. It is important to have lessons
learned in our lives. They teach us what we like,
and more importantly, what we do not like.

Expressing your own emotions without training of any kind is an altruistic disarray inside and outside your mind. If you aren't paying attention, you will not only get hurt, but you will hurt others.

What we fail to realize in our youth, is that we are not
machines. We are not products of our parents,
or the system. We are a product of the decisions
that we make, regardless of the result of
circumstances around us.

We may fall, falter, and shatter at some point.
Maybe we shatter multiple times throughout
our time on this Earth. Our spirit is challenged,
questioned, and of course broken. Then we get up,
repair, rebuild, and move forward to the next challenge.
We are resilient, and we are strong inside and out.

I feel like it is our jobs as humans to learn, rewire, and always work toward being the best person that we can be.

Each day is a new day, and we must embrace each day as a way to learn more about ourselves.

We are works in progress.
No matter what your age is,
you are a work in progress.
You are never "complete",
so stop looking for that.

No matter what you crawl through, where you fall, it matters most how you come out on the other side.

We fall down, we stand up, we run, we trip, we crawl;
we just have to remember to never stop.

Embrace your days,
your moments and your experiences.

Everyone has a hope and dream.
Everyone has a fear,
or a concern about themselves or life.
Everyone has lied.
Everyone lies in some context,
intentionally or inadvertently.
Everyone is similar to you, they breathe,
they laugh, they cry.
Everyone is like everyone else in some way.

Finding words of life, within itself,
shed light where darkness hides upon a shelf.

My awakening uncovered some truly devoted friends, and in this process I had to discard several not-so-true friends and enablers that needed to become forsaken in my path toward the light and out of this present darkness. This was an initial clearing of negative that allowed me to find my path once more.

Never assume that when you stop traveling down a bumpy road, that the new road won't be just as bumpy, the bumps just appear differently.

I had to take the longest, ugliest, most painful look
into the mirror than I had ever done before.

Wounds replaced patches, and scars formed over the madness and shame. Tangling all of the resent and unhappiness into a maddening menagerie of pain, anger, hurt and destruction is enough to kill anyone inside of their minds.

The storm is created to put you through something that
you would never ordinarily go though.
You will survive, but you will never be the same.

We just simply become who we are as we grow and
learn. Our paths change, our minds develop,
and our values adjust.

Don't let your relationship come to an abrupt
unexpected stop in the middle of the train tracks.
That powerful crash can not only disarm you or your
significant other, and it can cause irreparable heartache
and pain. It can destroy with ease, so take caution in
how long you wait to make that decision.

Begin like it's the beginning of an ending.

It is our own cognition that determines who we are,
or who we could be, and how we get there.
No one is to blame for your sadness, no one is
to blame for unhappiness any more than happiness
itself. These are emotions and feelings that we choose
to allow into our lives. We control how we react to
things. We are the messengers inside of our body
that dictate what the exterior expresses.

It is difficult to recognize that only you truly control you. No one else controls you. Life happens, no matter what – you cannot control others and they cannot control you.

Don't let go of the knowledge and understanding
that you make the decisions of the fabric
and the thread that creates your life.

Be aware of where you are, who you are, and what is motivating you. Then push yourself and do it.

You can wallow, or you can stand up and try again.
You are not a tree, you are not a stone,
you are not permanent.

No matter what decision you ever make, it won't be easy. You have to live with your decisions and choices. No one else is responsible for your happiness but you.

Our biggest strength lies inside of us, not around us.

I have discovered through my life, through happiness, sadness, pain, divorce, kids... happiness is certainly inside us. We have to find it and cultivate that beam of light into a massive ball of energy.

Happiness, as a state of mind, is yours for the making
and taking. Create it, embrace it, and then share it.

There are many times in our lives that we miss out
on an opportunity, an opportunity to just walk away
from something. If you are being disrespected,
treated unfairly, then walk away. One of the most
powerful things you could do in our life is know how
and when to give up, and just walk away for
the sake of preserving your personal values and sanity.

You do not need to be impolite or disrespectful
just because someone else chooses to be.

Our values, which fluctuate throughout our lives,
help to define our views and goals.
They are what we essentially live for each day.

Like plastic, we are firm yet pliable.
We are moldable throughout our existence.

I really wish that people would stop trying
to define normal. There isn't a human being
rule book anywhere that I have ever seen.

What you deem normal, may not be the same as what someone else deems normal. Remember that, and be your own 'normal'.

Everyone has a separate set of personal values
and not everyone's values look the same.

You are entitled to your views,
just as others are entitled to theirs.

As humans, we have a natural mode of bringing our own perception to experiences.

Adaptability is often key to survival.

"It is better to keep your mouth shut and look like a fool then to open it and remove all doubt." – Unknown

It is very valuable to realize what you are feeling at the moment you are in a conversation with someone else.

You will hopefully be on this Earth for many years
to come, so take a moment and appreciate
the moment that you are in. Each moment that we
experience will repeat itself, in one instance or another,
throughout our lives. We can learn so much from just
one moment, often without even realizing it.

Confidence, shyness, apprehension, ego,
it all comes to light in only a matter of seconds
if you're paying attention.

I believe whole-heartedly that the aphorism from Aristotle, "knowing yourself is the beginning of wisdom", holds very true. Knowing yourself can be one of the most powerful things you could ever acquire.

Life is a journey, through many great and not so great moments. Moments that we cherish, moments that we wish never happened, and moments that we take for granted. Moments of impact.

We must learn to breathe.. to be brittle.. to feel broken.
Because until then, we cannot learn to be whole again.

Life will end because it's temporary, so I embrace the moments in between the light and dark, and I hold on to everything with bloody hands of paths I've chosen.

These moments don't define exactly who you are,
they are merely building blocks in the complex being
that you are. They are pieces of the beauty and
magnificent universe you live in. Harness every moment,
good and bad, because these moments carve paths,
and what you learn from these moments can help
to guide you down any path you choose.

It is so easy to let others dictate our paths for us,
but it is not always what resonates in our minds
and hearts. To be fulfilled, to truly feel whole,
you have to make your decisions and commit to them.
Regardless of the outcome.

Sometimes the bad things that happen could
be saving us from something even worse.
Sometimes the decisions we make are just
to clarify what we already knew.

The one thing that I have learned, is that
the negative moments of impact often leave scars
and we tend to remember them. But, there are a great
many happiness moments that we sometimes forget,
because happiness doesn't leave a scar.

Life is an inosculation of beauty and adoration...
you just have to be willing to see it, to feel it,
and to embrace it with everything inside of you.

Never underestimate the power of the universe. There
are people that enter your world for many different
reasons. Good, bad or indifferent, these people help
create energy in our lives. It is how we harness that
energy that makes the most difference.

Have you felt alone?
I am sure that you have.
Have you felt alone, and it was by your choice?
Have you felt alone, when it wasn't your choice?
Is alone a bad thing?
There is a difference between alone, and lonely.

We are all works in progress.
We are all standing on our own two feet,
but from time to time, we falter, we fall,
and we sit there looking up at where we just were.
Deciding if we should stand up in that same spot again,
or stand up in a different spot and start over.

It's time to start taking steps again.
To learn to walk again, on my own.
To learn to "be" again, to live, breathe, and believe.

It is never too late, for anything
- stop saying "LIFE IS HARD"
- what the hell are you comparing that to exactly?
Stop saying "YOLO" and "You only live once"...
You live each and every day, over and over again.
Every day is a new day.
YOU ONLY DIE ONCE.
Remember that, and make each day count.
Be you, the best you that you can be.

We all experience happiness and pain.
You can never have one without the other.
You can't know true loss (outside of relatives)
without true love and closeness.

I have had to look at myself in the mirror,
and I had no one but me to answer to,
confide in, and become more aware of.
We have all been hurt before,
and it is very easy to hold that hurt in,
and twist it around to become something more.
We push people, we hurt others, we get angry,
we feel depressed and misunderstood.

I have had to let go.
Material objects, people, feelings of anger
or low self-esteem, feelings of guilt, doubt,
and the feeling of overwhelming defeat.
It has taken all of this time to recognize that I am the
man inside the machine. I have far greater value in the
appreciation of life, than in the pain of struggling with life.

I have had to let go. I
am not the same me that I was a year ago,
or even several years ago. I am becoming myself,
more than ever. Being honest to me, because I have to
face me every day, and I am not lying to myself
or fooling myself anymore.

We make mistakes, but we don't need to live
with the pain of regret. Change what can be changed,
and release what cannot. Accept the things that won't
change. Believe that you can start tomorrow new,
all over again.

Make your happiness, feed your soul,
open your eyes. Stop wasting time pretending things
are just 'how they are'.

I am new.
I am inspired.
I am aware,
and I am motivated.
I AM ME.

Keep shining, and be the harmony
you desire in your own life.

It's amazing the things that we experience in our lives.
As children as well as adults, we have vast experiences
and we often forget about them, if only for a moment.
Some make more impacts than others.

Here is an excerpt about an impact in my life...

- - - - - - -

I stood for what felt like an hour,
but was in reality, mere moments, and then panic.
I had no more bullets in the gun, and I stood there
while it smoked in the moonlight and a light
flipped on in the house.

I ran, I ran hard and fast, feeling like someone
was chasing me to kill me as I had planned to kill them.
I felt cold and then hot and then scared
and then sick and then,
I just wanted to be home.

- - - - - - -

Oftentimes, the paths that we choose in our lives
are simply a product of the moment
in which we are engaged.
Take time to breathe in your moments
and be with them.

Never make a decision when you're angry,
never make a promise when you're happy,
and always take a moment to decide for yourself.
Because in the end, it is only yourself that can
truly choose the path that is best for you.

Live without regret,
and appreciate all of your moments.

It is the end of 2016...
the end of a year,
the end of moments that have carved pieces
into our lives, happy or painful,
meaningful, or things we'd rather forget.
Either way, it's over... we have made it.

Sometimes, it's difficult to put into words just what goes through our minds. We can be upset and angry, or happy and appreciative. We have so many feelings and thoughts that we keep to ourselves. They run through our minds day in and day out, and we often don't give a second thought to the minor things.

The things that we think, whether we are sitting at home, wondering why the hell there are so many commercials during our favorite shows, or when the dog is going to stop barking at the neighbors. Other times you're walking through the store, seeing the old couple still holding hands and shopping together, while, off in another aisle, someone is getting after their kids for being "too loud."

I speak about moments quite often, there are all types of these moments. Those moments when you realize the world around you, and that there are so many things happening all at once...

Never take your moments for granted, because some day, you won't have many of them left, and you never want to regret those moments that you let slip away.

Someone near you needs a hug, a friend needs a simple "how are you doing," and then, of course, your special someone... they need to be reminded how important they are to you, but also - let them know you appreciate them. Everyone needs appreciation.

I appreciate you for reading this. I appreciate those that are near and dear to me, and I hope that you let others know how much you appreciate them.

HOW I BEGAN WRITING MY NEW BOOK, "I AM"

My journey started over a year ago. It was a moment of impact and immediate change in my life. I had to take a step back, and then another, and finally a complete jump back and to the left.

I started to fall apart, which we all do at certain points in our lives. I felt like I had woken up from some strange dream, and the reality was far too painful to comprehend. I was beside myself, and alone.

I stripped everything away from my life at that point. Every materialistic item, my job, my home, vehicles, everything that I once held in my hands, had suddenly lost all meaning. So why did I need any of it?

I walked away from it all. I had to. I had to discover who I was inside of me, from the bottom to the top, inside and out. I needed to essentially pull down all the walls and learn how to rebuild them again.

I had to reevaluate my entire life, my complete being, to fully understand what pieces needed improving, and what pieces could remain.

I took the chance of walking away from everything, and starting all over, with nothing. 42 years old, and starting over, raw, feeling desolate, and just needing to find me again.

My new book is all about my experience and the things that went through my mind and the realizations I made and things that I have learned in the last year of my life throughout this whole process.

It has been very difficult, some days more than others. But I am standing, breathing, and taking life day by day and embracing it for what it is. The storms we weather make us stronger, and we are never the same person when we come out the other side.

THOUGHTS ABOUT THINKING

One of the things that I have wanted to convey, are the feelings and thoughts that pass through my mind. My mind is constantly 'on', rarely is it shut off, and oftentimes I have difficulty getting to sleep or staying asleep. I sleep well, once I can power down. Unfortunately, it often seeps into my dreams as well.

I have spent a great deal of time this last year digging through my mind, my soul, my heart, and my surroundings. I have met people that have been amazing and wonderful, and I have met some not so wonderful people. However, each person has taught me something about life or about myself.

In some way, I have discovered that every moment makes an impression on us and we often brush things aside. I don't want to do that any longer, so I am working constantly to pay attention to the moments and the little things that happen and are said each and every day.

I am working on not over-thinking everything. I have anxiety, I have ADD, and I suffer from depression. I am happy to say, that I have learned to come to terms with these and I have also made the decision to work on embracing and coping with these things.

They are not hampering my ability to live life. They just influence how I live it. I have been more cognitive of my thoughts and worries, and I work to continually improve my coping abilities. Focus is an important step in overcoming many of these.

Eating healthier, sleeping regularly, and becoming active are important steps in dealing with anxiety and depression. I choose to be happy, and although I have my setbacks and days, I continue to push forward because there is no real reason not to.

I have three beautiful daughters, whom I love tremendously, and they are a determining factor in many of my life's decisions. Not everyone agrees with me, not everyone appreciates what I write, what I say, or how I decide to live my life. But these decisions are not in the hands of others. They are in my hands only.

I love nature, and being outside, in nature is an amazingly refreshing experience. Hiking, walking, just being in the fresh air is wonderful and freeing. Taking in the trees, animals, and sky are focal points that help calm me from the inside out.

FLEETING ARE OUR MOMENTS IN LIFE

Never should we ignore the thoughts that enter our minds, as they are catalysts for action.

Breath in the air around you, and always listen to your mind, your heart, and your gut instincts. They may not always agree, but you can be sure that they always know.

It's easy to waste time in your life, staring at a clock, expecting something to happen that will not happen as long as you are expecting it to.

MOMENTS ARE MERE SNAPSHOTS IN OUR LIVES

Stop taking your moments for granted. Live each day with embracing arms and understanding that it could be your last, so make it your best.

EPILOGUE

Inspiration and motivation are important to me. They are pieces of positive influence, or words of thought that help me through a moment, or a day. They can often enter my mind multiple times and help to see me through some rough times.

I enjoy writing my own inspiration or quotes, as a way of helping others, to let them know that they are not alone on their journey through this mortal world of ours.

I always say that every day is a new day, but I also realize that some days and moments are longer than others. We often need to turn to others, whether we want to or not, for a calm moment, peace of mind, closure, hope, something to clutch onto.

Thank you for reading my words. I hope that you may gain something from these words. My books are a means of release for me, and hopefully a connection for you. Cherish and embrace your moments in life.

-J Christian Connett

ABOUT THE AUTHOR

Christian Connett is a Digital Marketing Architect, Strategist, Author and Speaker. His speaking topics include Contextual Behavior, Cognitive Behavior, Interpersonal Relationships, Psychology in Marketing, and Personality in the Workplace. Christian also conducts workshops for Digital Marketing and Interpersonal Relationships.

Christian's experience includes Consulting & Coaching, Adjunct College Instruction, Workshop development, Public Speaking, and of course authoring books.

THE
END

Made in the USA
Middletown, DE
02 February 2022